Math is
Coloring Easter Book

Learn to count
and add
in a very simple way.
Age 2-5

Math is Fun. Coloring Easter Book.

Learn to count and add in a very simple way. Age 2-5

The addition is explained in such a way that small children or those with learning difficulties quickly understand and love math.

Your child can begin developing from a young age. If a child trains their memory, drawing, reading, and the ability to associate from a young age, your child will be better at school.

Spend ten minutes a day with books with your child.
It is an investment in the future of your child.

Good luck.
See my other great books for kids, just look on amazon and look at the authors-name
"Susanna Petri"
To find more books

Three

Four

Five

Seven

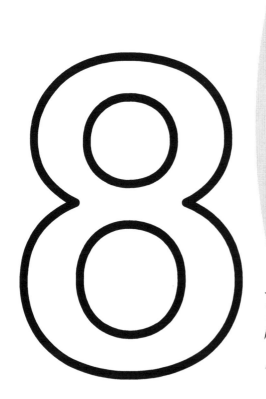

Nine

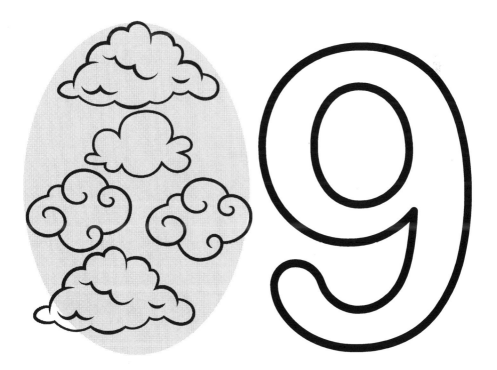

Ten

10

Eleven

11

Twelve

12

Thirteen

13

Fourteen

14

Fifteen

15

Sixteen

16

Seventeen

Eighteen

Nineteen

Twenty

20

$$1 + 1 =$$

$+$ $=$

$$1 + 2 =$$

$+$ $=$

1+3 =

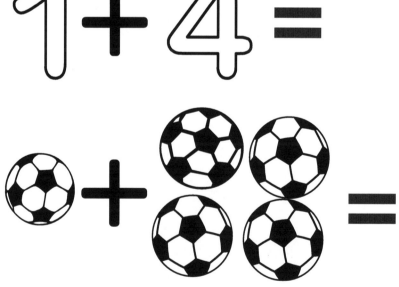

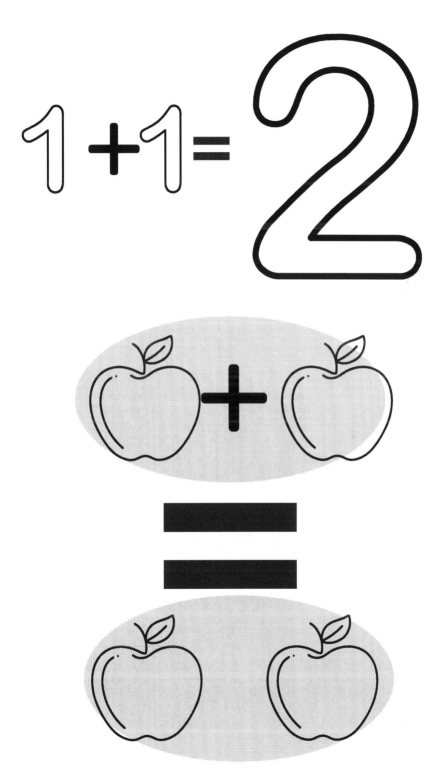

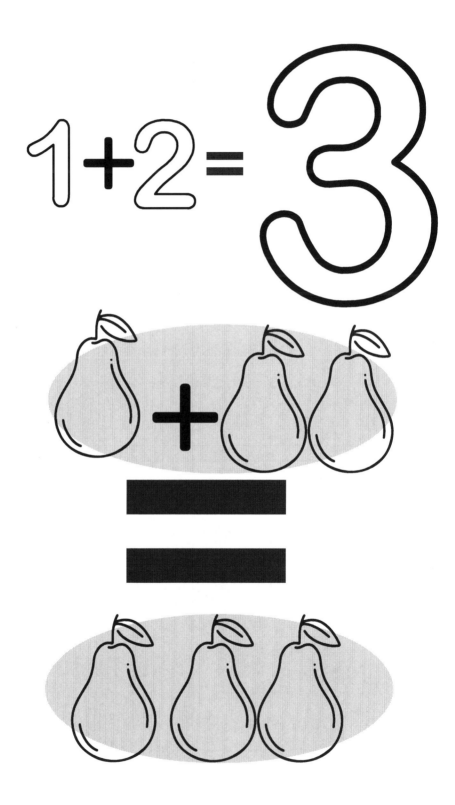

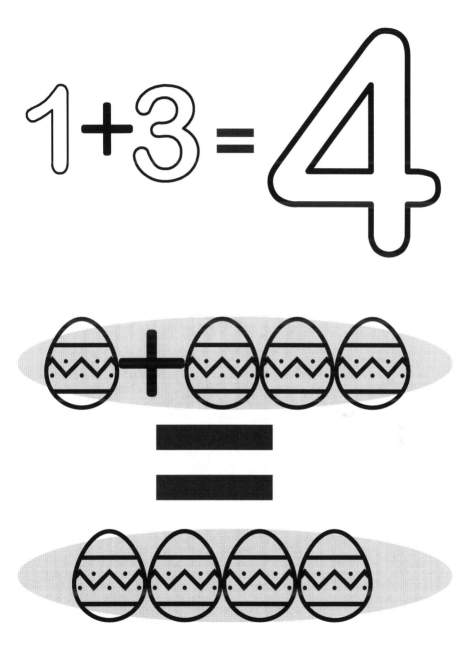

1+4=5

1 + 5 =

+ =

---

2 + 1 =

+ =

2+2=

+ =

2+3 =

+ =

1+5=6

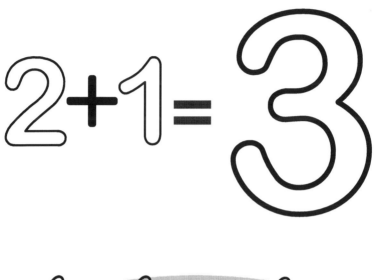

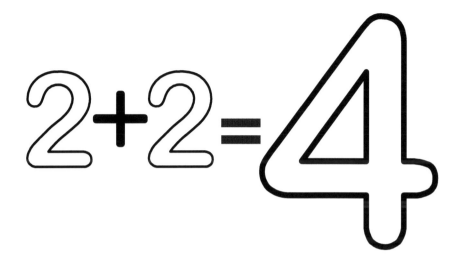

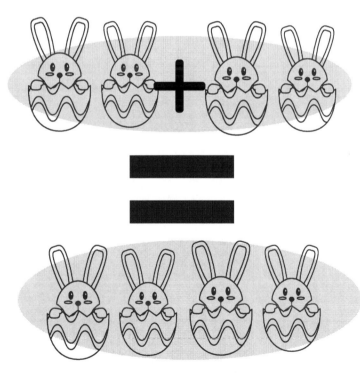

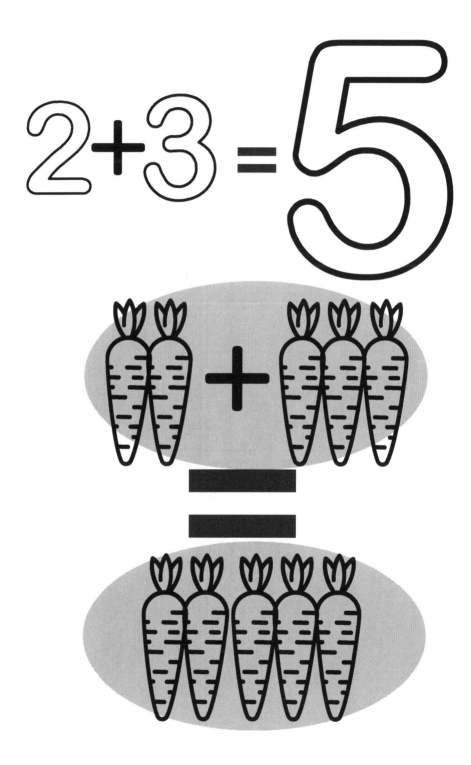

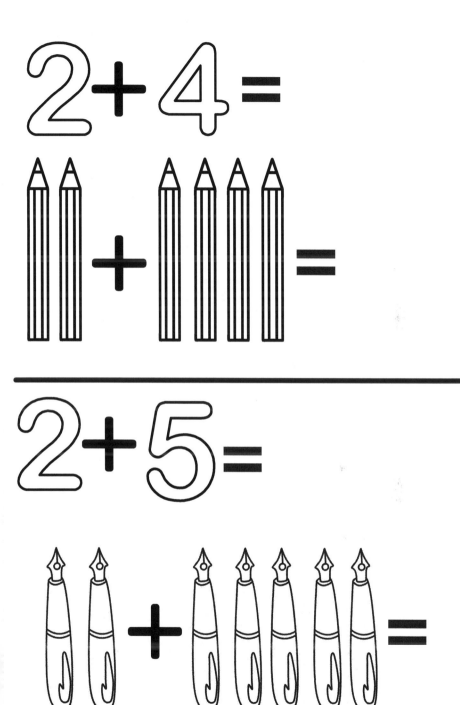

3+1=

3+2=

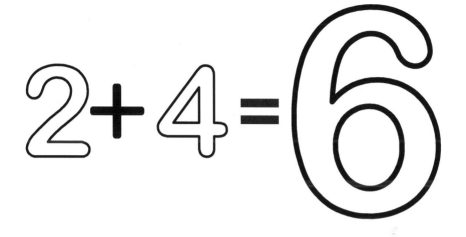

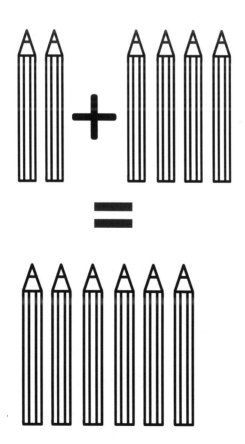

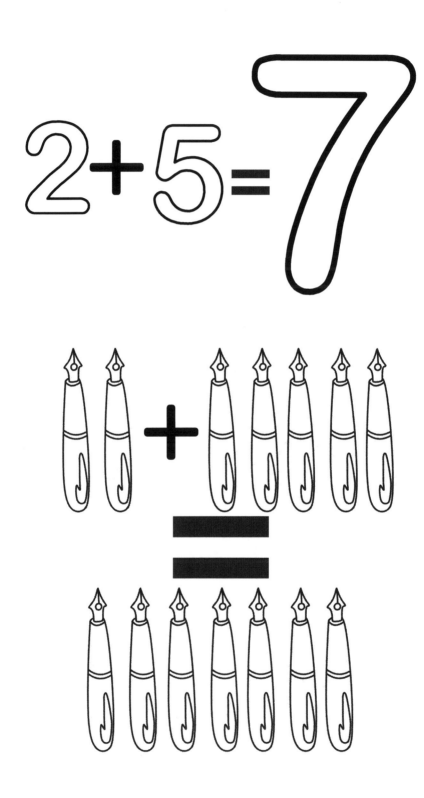

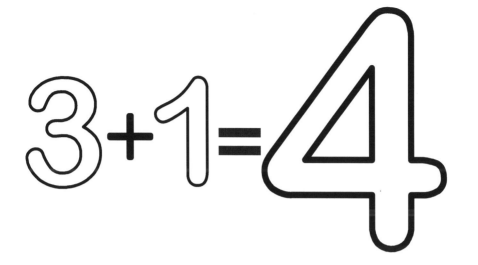

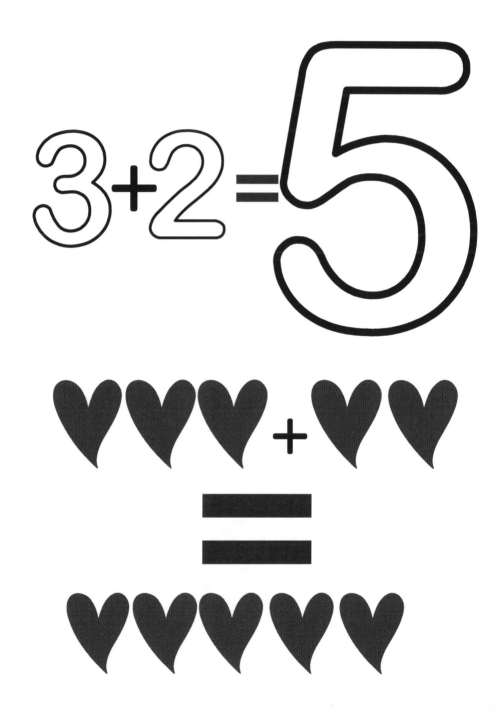

3+3=

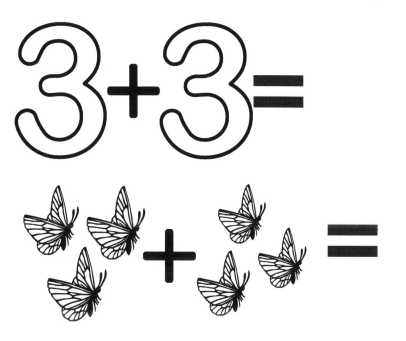

3+4=

3+5=

+ =

4+1=

+ =

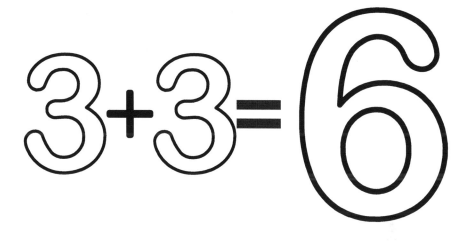

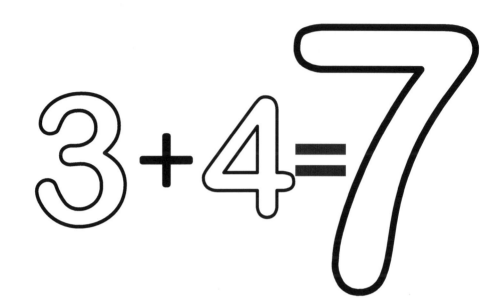

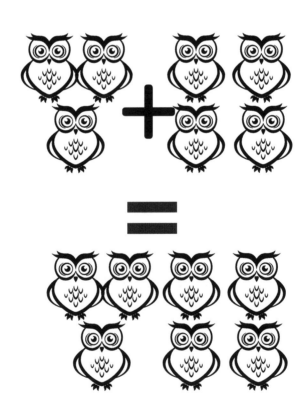

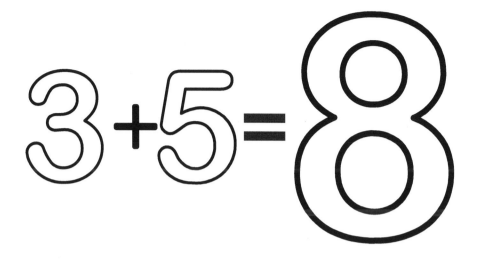

4+2=

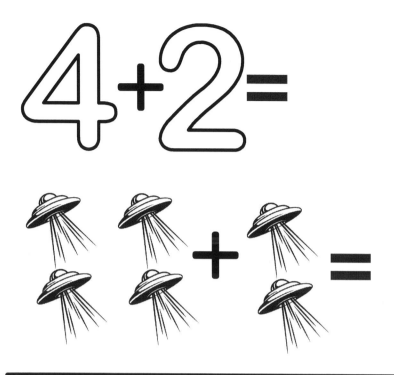

4+3=

4+4=

_____

4+5=

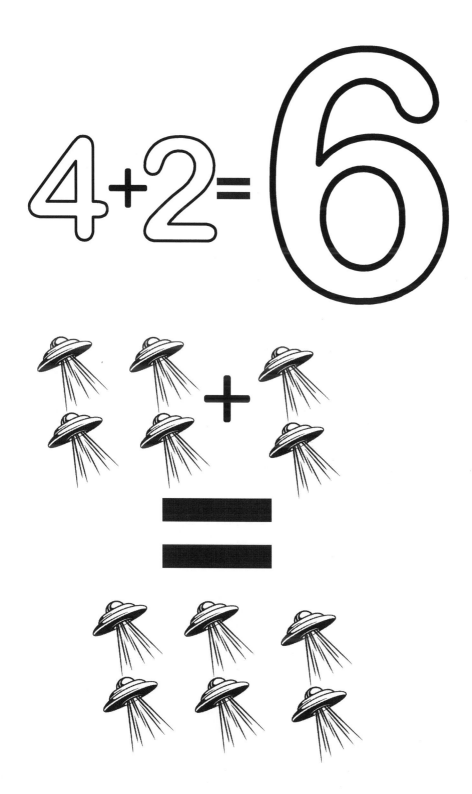

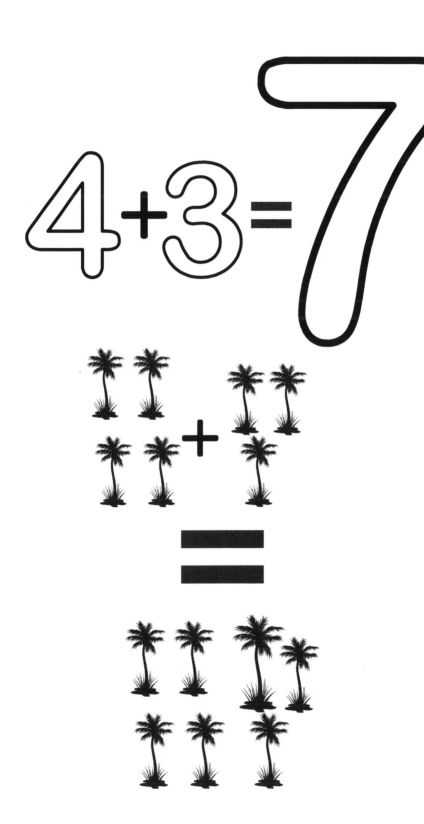

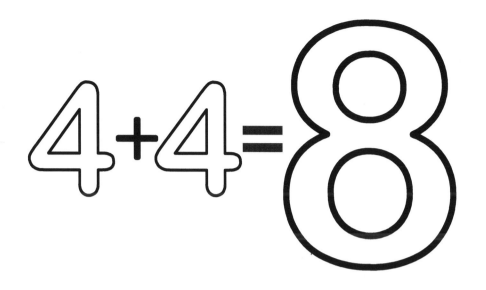

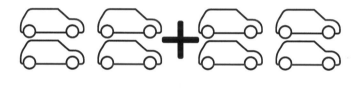

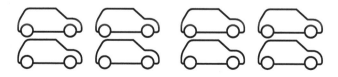

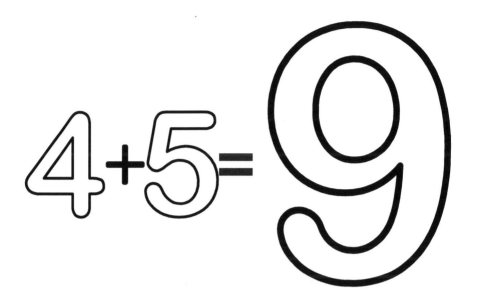

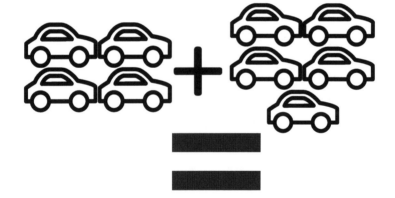

5+1=

+ =

5+2=

+ =

5+3=

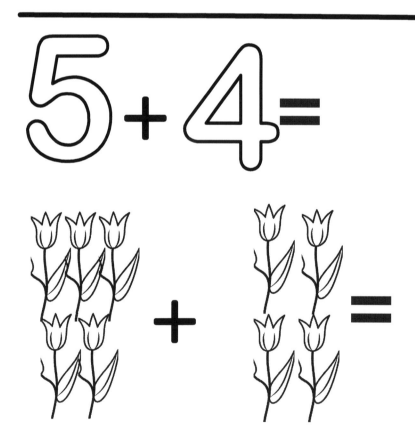

5 + 3 =

5+4=

5+5=

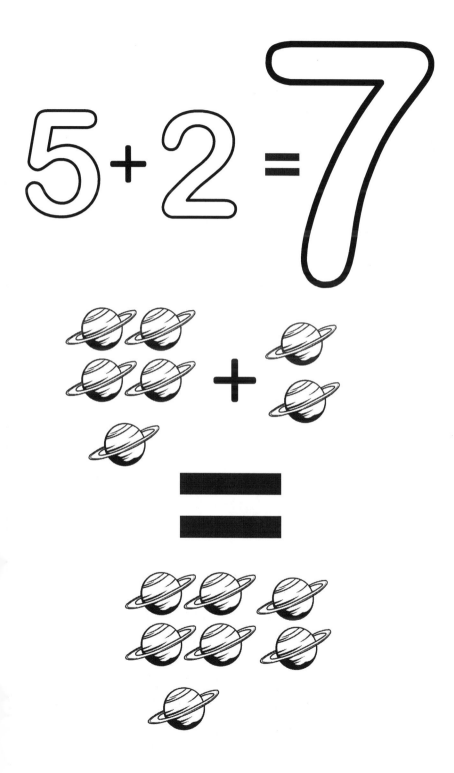

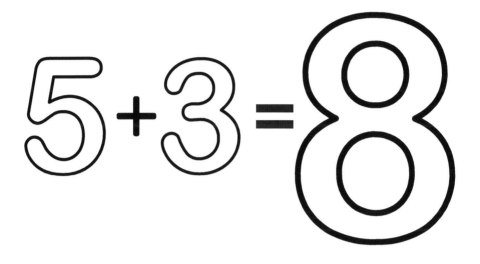

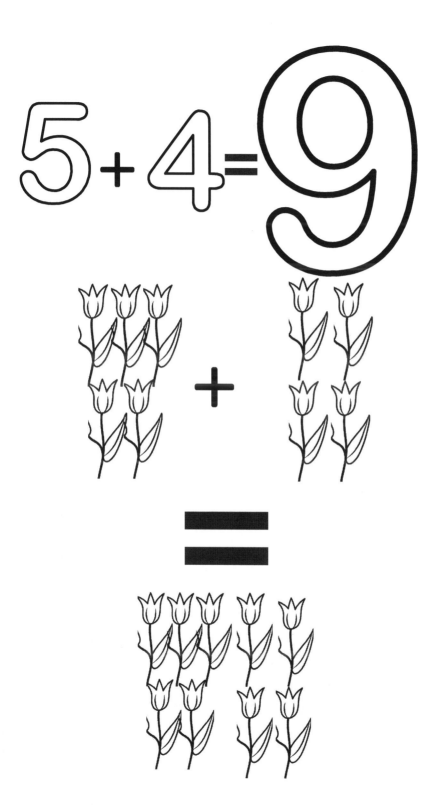

5+5=10

1 + 1 =

1 + 2 =

1 + 3 =

1 + 4 =

1 + 5 =

2 + 1 =

2 + 2 =

2 + 3 =

2 + 4 =

2 + 5 =

3 + 1 =

3 + 2 =

3 + 3 =

3 + 4 =

3 + 5 =

4 + 1 =

4 + 2 =

4 + 3 =

4 + 4 =

4 + 5 =

5 + 1 =

5 + 2 =

5 + 3 =

5 + 4 =

5 + 5 =

1 + 4 =

3 + 2 =

2 + 1 =

4 + 2 =

1 + 1 =

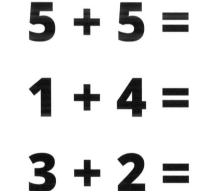

2 + 4 =

4 + 2 =

5 + 3 =

3 + 5 =

1 + 5 =

5 + 1 =

2 + 3 =

3 + 2 =

4 + 1 =

1 + 4 =

Well done, you are a math master

Keep it up

Math is great fun

Thank you for buying
the math coloring
book
and have fun.

Printed in Great Britain
by Amazon

32459623R00037